Scary and Savage Planet

Interactive Quiz

Managing Editors: Simon Melhuish and Sarah Wells

Series Editor: Nikole G Bamford

Designer: Linley J Clode

Writer: Nick Daws

Cover Design: Radio

Published by
The Lagoon Group
PO Box 311, KT2 5QW, UK
PO Box 990676, Boston, MA 02199, USA

ISBN: 1904797571

© LAGOON BOOKS 2004

Lagoon Books is a trade mark of
Lagoon Trading Company Limited.
All rights reserved.

www.intelliquestbooks.com

Printed in China

IntelliQuest

UNIQUE BOOK CODE	013

Instructions

First of all make sure you
have a Quizmo –

Find the book's unique code (this
appears at the top of this page).
Use the < and > buttons to scroll
to this number on the Quizmo screen.
Press the ⏎ button to enter the
code, and you're ready to go.

Use the < > scroll buttons to select
the question number you want to
answer. Press the A, B, C, or D
button to enter your chosen answer.

If you are correct the green light beside
the button you pressed will flash. You can then
use the scroll button to move on to another question.

If your answer is incorrect, the red light beside the
button you pressed will flash.

Don't worry, you can try again and again until you have the correct answer, OR move on to another question. (Beware: the more times you guess incorrectly, the lower your final percentage score will be!)

You can finish the quiz at any point – just press the ⬅ button to find out your score and rank as follows:

75% or above	You're a force to be reckoned with!
50% – 74%	You're a whirlwind of wisdom!
25% – 49%	Did that tidal wave catch you unawares?
Less than 25%	0.001 on the Richter scale. You're a natural disaster!

If you do press the ⬅ button to find out your score, this will end your session and you will have to use the ⬅ to start again!

HAVE FUN!

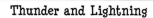
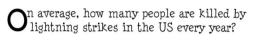

001

On average, how many people are killed by lightning strikes in the US every year?

A) 12
B) 55
C) 90
D) 150

002

Which US state has the most thunderstorms?

A) Florida
B) Arkansas
C) Wisconsin
D) Texas

003

About how many times a year is the Empire State building in New York struck by lightning?

A) 10
B) 50
C) 100
D) 200

Thunder and Lightning

In recent years, people doing which of the following activities have been killed by lightning?

    A) Mowing a lawn
    B) Loading a truck
    C) Watering plants
    D) All of these

You can tell how close a storm is to you by counting the number of seconds between seeing a lightning bolt and hearing the thunder. What is the distance of the storm for each second?

    A) 100 meters/300 feet
    B) 200 meters/600 feet
    C) 300 meters/900 feet
    D) 400 meters/1200 feet

How hot does a lightning bolt get?
    A) 30,000° C/54032° F
    B) 10,000° C/18032° F
    C) 50,000° C/90032° F
    D) 1,000° C/1832° F

007

Where is the safest place to be during a lightning storm?

    A) Under a tall tree
    B) In a house
    C) In the middle of a field
    D) Lying face down on the ground

008

How many volts does it take for a cloud-to-ground lightning strike to occur?

    A) 100 million to 1 billion
    B) 10 million to 100 million
    C) 1 million to 10 million
    D) 100,000 to 1 million

009

Which of these things should you avoid during a thunderstorm?

    A) Reading a book
    B) Eating a pizza
    C) Using the phone
    D) Doing your homework

How is thunder produced?

A) By the rapid expansion of air

B) By static electricity popping your eardrums

C) By two or more clouds colliding

D) By the actions of the thunder gods

010

How many people died in the so-called Storm of the Century which hit the eastern United States in March 1993?

A) 1,080

B) 762

C) 243

D) 104

011

Which electrical charge collects at the bottom of thunderclouds?

A) Positive

B) Negative

C) Neutral

D) Explosive

012

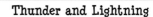

013 About how many thunderstorms occur across the world every day?

A) 25,000
B) 44,000
C) 51,000
D) 60,000

014 An average thunderstorm releases the energy equivalent of:

A) 100 car crashes
B) A Sidewinder missile
C) A 20 kiloton nuclear weapon
D) An exploding star

015 Ball lightning is the name given to floating balls of light or electricity often observed during or after thunderstorms. The lightning appears to be self-contained in a spherical formation. What causes it?

A) High Voltage Power Lines emitting excess charge
B) Nitrogen Plasma exploding after an electrical storm
C) Nobody knows
D) Microwaves impacting on each other causing light

Which of the following has ball lightning not been known to do?

A) It has been known to melt walls
B) It has been known to cook a chicken on contact
C) It has been known to kill people
D) It has been known to be white, yellow, red or green

016

The greatest number of people who die from being struck by lightning are...

A) Golfers
B) Farmers
C) Fishermen
D) Teachers

017

What is the correct name for thunderclouds?

A) Cumulus
B) Stratocumulus
C) Cumulonimbus
D) Cirrus

018

Deserts and Dust Storms

019 Which is reckoned to be the driest desert in the world, with average yearly rainfall of less than half an inch?

- **A)** Atacama
- **B)** Kalahari
- **C)** Sahara
- **D)** Namib

020 Which desert contains the world's longest expanse of unbroken sand?

- **A)** Kalahari
- **B)** Gobi
- **C)** Mojave
- **D)** Arabian

021 Dust storms originating in Saharan Africa have increased ten-fold over the past 50 years. What is believed to be a major cause of this?

- **A)** Global warming
- **B)** Use of vehicles rather than camels to cross the desert
- **C)** Acid rain
- **D)** The hole in the ozone layer

Up to what height can dust be carried by a dust storm?

A) 16,000 feet/4878 meters
B) 11,000 feet/3354 meters
C) 8,000 feet/2439 meters
D) 5,000 feet/1524 meters

`022`

What damaging effects have been attributed to Saharan dust storms?

A) Melting of the ice-caps
B) Respiratory diseases
C) Destruction of coral reefs
D) All of these

`023`

What is the average size of Saharan dust storms?

A) 200 km/124 miles across
B) 100 km/62 miles across
C) 500 km/310 miles across
D) 50 km/31 miles across

`024`

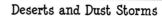

025

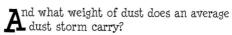

And what weight of dust does an average dust storm carry?

    A) 20 tons
    B) 50 tons
    C) 100 tons
    D) 200 tons

026

How high are the grains of sand normally whipped up in a sandstorm?

    A) 30 feet/15.3 meters
    B) 20 feet/6.1 meters
    C) 6 feet/1.8 meters
    D) 4 feet/1.2 meters

027

Deserts can be cold as well as hot. Which of these is a cold desert?

    A) Great Basin
    B) Kalahari
    C) Thar
    D) Ice cream sundae

Deserts and Dust Storms

How long do sandstorms normally last?

A) Less than a day
B) 1 to 4 days
C) 3 to 5 days
D) About a week

If you were in Death Valley - hopefully with plenty of chilled drinks - which desert would you be in?

A) Mojave
B) Sonoran
C) Great Basin
D) Monte

Takla Makan is a desert in Western China. What does the name Takla Makan mean in English?

A) Place of no return
B) Give me water
C) Too darned hot
D) Futility

031

How does a tsunami differ from a tidal wave?

A) It has nothing to do with tides
B) A tidal wave is influenced by the moon, a tsunami by Mars
C) It's bigger
D) It doesn't - it's the same thing

032

What does the word tsunami mean in Japanese?

A) Harbor wave
B) Divine wind
C) Wave of terror
D) Mexican wave

033

Which US state is statistically most likely to be hit by a tsunami?

A) Alaska
B) California
C) Florida
D) Hawaii

Terrible Tsunamis

Which of these is a warning sign of a tsunami?

034

A) Strange lights are seen in the sky
B) Pets begin to act nervously
C) Water suddenly rushes from the shore out to sea
D) People run around screaming

What are the most common causes of a tsunami?

035

A) Volcanic eruptions
B) Earthquakes and landslides
C) Meteorite strikes
D) Sea monsters fighting

Where was the highest recorded tsunami?

036

A) Honolulu, Hawaii
B) Flores Island, Indonesia
C) Lituya Bay, Alaska
D) Loch Ness, Scotland

037

And how high was it?

A) 20,000 feet/6,096 meters
B) 300 feet/914 meters
C) 1,800 feet/549 meters
D) 1,300 feet/396 meters

038

What is the average speed of a tsunami in the deep ocean?

A) 100-150 mph/161-241 kph
B) 300-400 mph/483-644 kph
C) 1,000-1,200 mph/1610-1932 kph
D) 500-600 mph/805-966 kph

039

And what is the average height of a tsunami in the deep ocean?

A) 16 inches/41 cm
B) 100 feet/30.5 meters
C) 200 feet/61 meters
D) 400 feet/122 meters

Terrible Tsunamis

How far apart are the waves of a tsunami as it travels across the deep ocean?

A) 10 miles/16 km
B) 1,000 miles/1609 km
C) 100 miles/161 km
D) 5,000 miles/8047 km

040

An earthquake occurring 30 miles/48 km below the seabed can cause a tsunami. What magnitude on the Richter scale must it have?

A) 5.0
B) 5.5
C) 6.0
D) 6.5

041

What percent of tsunami warnings issued since 1948 have been false alarms?

A) 25%
B) 40%
C) 75%
D) 95%

042

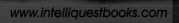

043

What happens to the height of a tsunami as it approaches the shore?

   A) Remains constant
   B) Decreases
   C) Increases
   D) Might do any of these

044

And what happens to the speed of a tsunami as it approaches the shore?

   A) Might do any of the following
   B) Does not change
   C) Speeds up
   D) Slows down

045

Probably the most destructive tsunami occurred after the eruption of which volcano in 1883?

   A) Stromboli
   B) Krakatoa
   C) Etna
   D) Vesuvius

Snow and Blizzards

What proportion of the Earth's surface is covered by permanent snow and ice?

A) 8%
B) 12%
C) 15%
D) 20%

On average, how many inches of snow are required to produce one inch of water?

A) One inch
B) Three inches
C) Ten inches
D) Twelve inches

What is graupel?

A) A sensational new boy band
B) Snowflakes composed of many individual ice crystals
C) Rounded, well-bonded snow that is older than one year
D) Snowflakes that become round pellets due to ice forming on them

049

Which is the only permanent snowcap within sight of the Equator?

A) Mount Everest
B) Mount Kilimanjaro
C) Mount Annapurna
D) Mount Rushmore

050

How high does the wind speed have to become and how low the visibility before a snowfall is officially regarded as a blizzard?

A) 40 mph, 1/2 mile
B) 30 mph, 1/2 mile
C) 40 mph, 1/4 mile
D) 35 mph, 1/4 mile

051

The biggest recorded snowfall in a single day was 75.8 inches/193 cm on April 14-15, 1921. Where did this occur?

A) Silver Lake, Colorado
B) Mont Blanc, France
C) Saratoga Springs, New York
D) Mount Erebus, Antarctica

How many sides do most snow crystals have?

A) 4

B) 5

C) 6

D) 8

052

A single snowstorm can drop 40 million tons of snow. That is the energy equivalent of:

A) A 10 ton truck traveling all the way from New York to San Francisco

B) A short order cook frying 10,000 burgers

C) 120 atomic bombs

D) A supernova

053

Snow rollers are a very rare phenomenon, where giant snowballs are formed naturally by strong winds blowing across a flat, snow-covered field. Around what temperature does it have to be for snow rollers to form?

A) -20° C/-4° F

B) 0° C/32° F

C) -10° C/14° F

D) 5° C/41° F

054

055

On December 18, 2000, large numbers of snow rollers were seen in Russell County, Kansas. The biggest ones were equal in size to:

A) Skittles
B) 30-gallon drums
C) Basketballs
D) Satellite launchers

056

Where was the largest-ever snowflake found?

A) Bratsk, Siberia
B) Mount Erebus, Antarctica
C) Silver Lake, Colorado
D) Reykjavik, Iceland

057

And how big was it?

A) 6 by 8 inches/15 by 20 cm
B) 7 by 9 inches/18 by 23 cm
C) 8 by 12 inches/20 by 30 cm
D) 10 by 14 inches/25 by 36 cm

The snow in Fairbanks, Alaska is unusually dry. How much does it take to make one inch of water?

058

- **A)** 10 inches
- **B)** 12 inches
- **C)** 15 inches
- **D)** 20 inches

Rochester, New York is the snowiest large city in the United States. What is its average annual snowfall?

059

- **A)** 72 inches/183 cm
- **B)** 83 inches/211 cm
- **C)** 94 inches/239 cm
- **D)** 105 inches/267 cm

On average, how many snow-producing storms affect the continental United States each year?

060

- **A)** 85
- **B)** 95
- **C)** 105
- **D)** 125

061

What is the typical snow-producing lifetime of these storms?

A) 1 to 3 days
B) 2 to 5 days
C) 3 to 6 days
D) 4 to 7 days

062

Which of these is NOT a real term coined by skiers to describe a certain type of snow?

A) Onion soup
B) Corduroy
C) Mashed potatoes
D) Champagne powder

063

What percentage of the world's fresh water is locked up as snow or ice?

A) 50%
B) 60%
C) 80%
D) 95%

Snow and Blizzards

Why does salt help stop snow turning into ice?

- **A)** Salt makes snow evaporate faster
- **B)** Salt water needs to be much colder to freeze
- **C)** Salt turns snow into a soft powder
- **D)** Salt has magical powers

064

Up to how long have sheep been known to survive after being buried in snowdrifts?

- **A)** 2 weeks
- **B)** 5 days
- **C)** 3 days
- **D)** 12 hours

065

The Rocky Mountains are reckoned to be among the snowiest places on Earth. What is their average annual snowfall?

- **A)** 200-300 inches/508-762 cm
- **B)** 500-600 inches/1270-1524 cm
- **C)** 400-500 inches/1016-1270 cm
- **D)** 300-400 inches/762-1016 cm

066

067

An avalanche is a mass of snow sliding down a mountainside. When do most avalanches occur?

A) No special time
B) Just before large snowstorms
C) During periods of fine weather
D) During or just after large snowstorms

068

At what angle of slope do 90% of all avalanches start?

A) 10 to 25
B) 20 to 35
C) 30 to 45
D) 40 to 60

069

At what speed do avalanches typically travel?

A) Up to 60 mph/96 kph
B) Up to 40 mph/64 kph
C) Up to 30 mph/48 kph
D) Up to 50 mph/80 kph

Avalanches and Landslides

What was the speed of the fastest
avalanche ever recorded?

070

A) 170 mph/273 kph
B) 186 mph/300 kph
C) 207 mph/333 kph
D) 217 mph/349 kph

And in which country did this occur?

071

A) Chile
B) Switzerland
C) Austria
D) Canada

An avalanche made up of ice fell over 10,000
feet from a mountain in the Andes in
Peru. In the space of 15 minutes, how many
people and livestock did it kill?

072

A) 1,500 people and 5,000 livestock
B) 2,500 people and 8,000 livestock
C) 4,500 people and 20,000 livestock
D) 3,500 people and 10,000 livestock

073

About how long can most people survive if caught in an avalanche?

A) 20 minutes
B) 30 minutes
C) 45 minutes
D) 1 hour

074

How long did a postman in Austria - believed to be the record-holder - survive after being caught in an avalanche?

A) 12 hours
B) 3 days
C) 5 days
D) A week

075

What is the total financial cost of landslide damage every year in the USA?

A) $0.5 billion
B) $1 billion
C) $2 billion
D) $3 billion

Avalanches and Landslides

Which of these weather conditions is most likely to produce a landslide?

A) A short period of torrential rain

B) A long spell of exceptionally hot weather

C) Slow, steady rainfall over a long period

D) A long spell of exceptionally cold weather

076

Debris flows are like mud avalanches. Up to what speed can they move?

A) Over 100 mph/161 kph

B) Over 80 mph/129 kph

C) Over 60 mph/97 kph

D) Over 120 mph/193 kph

077

In a record-breaking storm in the San Francisco area in January 1982, how many debris flows were triggered during a single night?

A) Over 18,000

B) Over 15,000

C) Over 12,000

D) Over 10,000

078

079

And what was the total value of the property damage caused?

A) Over $45 million
B) Over $53 million
C) Over $66 million
D) Over $82 million

080

Which of these natural phenomena can also result in debris flows?

A) Drought
B) Fog
C) Wildfire
D) Heatwave

081

Which of these statements about landslides is NOT true?

A) Landslides occur in every state of the USA
B) Landslides never occur in the same place twice
C) If you live on a hill, you are likely to be at an increased risk
D) They often occur with little or no warning

What is the coldest temperature ever measured on Antarctica?

082

- **A)** -48.5° C/-55.3° F
- **B)** -89.2° C/-128.6° F
- **C)** -76.4° C/-105.5° F
- **D)** -56.7° C/-70.1° F

What is Deception Island, off the coast of the Antarctic Peninsula, famous for?

083

- **A)** It appears and disappears with the tide
- **B)** It's the southernmost island in the world
- **C)** It's warm enough to swim there
- **D)** It's an optical illusion - it doesn't really exist

The magnetic North Pole moves from year to year, and even from day to day. How far has it moved in the last 200 years?

084

- **A)** 480 km/298 miles
- **B)** 760 km/472 miles
- **C)** 1,100 km/683 miles
- **D)** 1,500 km/932 miles

085 If the magnetic North Pole keeps moving at its present speed and direction, where will it be in fifty years?

- **A)** Greenland
- **B)** Iceland
- **C)** New York
- **D)** Siberia

086 The ALH 84-001 meteorite was named after the area of Antarctica in which it was found, the Allan Hills. What is the meteorite's claim to fame?

- **A)** It was the first artificial meteorite
- **B)** It is the best evidence yet of life on Mars
- **C)** It is the largest known meteorite
- **D)** It is made of a previously unknown substance

087 In the Arctic Circle you can see a phenomenon called the Northern Lights. By what other name are they known?

- **A)** Sky lights
- **B)** Aurora Australis
- **C)** Aurora Borealis
- **D)** Neon rain

Mount Waialeale in Hawaii is reckoned to be the wettest place in the USA. On average, how many days a year does rain fall there?

A) 280
B) 335
C) 350
D) 415

088

About how many cloud droplets have to come together to produce one raindrop?

A) 1,000
B) 10,000
C) 100,000
D) 1,000,000

089

What is the world's one-minute rainfall record?

A) 0.55 inches/1.4 cm
B) 0.82 inches/2.1 cm
C) 1.23 inches/3.1 cm
D) 1.56 inches/4 cm

090

Rain and Hail

091

And where in the USA did this occur in July 1956?

A) Orlando, Florida
B) Saratoga Springs, New York
C) Silver Lake, Colorado
D) Unionville, Maryland

092

The record for the greatest recorded rainfall in a year is held by Assam in India. How much rain fell there in 1880-81?

A) 1,041 inches/26.4 meters
B) 859 inches/21.8 meters
C) 732 inches/18.6 meters
D) 546 inches/13.9 meters

093

Where on Earth does the most hail fall in one year?

A) Christchurch, New Zealand
B) Nuuk, Greenland
C) Helsinki, Finland
D) Keriche, Kenya

And how many days a year on average does hail fall there?

A) 132 days

B) 102 days

C) 152 days

D) 182 days

094

The record for the greatest rainfall in a day is held by La Reunion in the Indian Ocean. How much rain fell there on March 15, 1952?

A) 89.56 inches/227.5 cm

B) 105.59 inches/268.2 cm

C) 73.62 inches/187 cm

D) 65.43 inches/166.2 cm

095

The largest hailstone ever known to fall in the USA was found in Aurora, Nebraska on June 22, 2003. What was its total circumference?

A) 9.25 inches/23.5 cm

B) 11.50 inches/29.2 cm

C) 18.75 inches/47.6 cm

D) 14.50 inches/36.5 cm

096

097

At what speed do hailstones normally fall to Earth?

A) 70-100 mph/113-160 kph
B) 50-70 mph/80-113 kph
C) 30-50 mph/48-80 kph
D) 100-130 mph/160-210 kph

098

The heaviest hailstones on record fell in the Gopalganj district of Bangladesh on April 14, 1986. How much did the biggest weigh?

A) 1.2 lbs
B) 1.5 lbs
C) 2.2 lbs
D) 2.8 lbs

099

And how many people are recorded to have died in that hailstorm?

A) 114
B) 54
C) 126
D) 92

Rain and Hail

Which US state has the most hail every year?

    A) Nevada
    B) Alaska
    C) Colorado
    D) Arizona

What is the longest time a rainbow is known to have lasted?

    A) 3 hours
    B) 68 minutes
    C) 90 minutes
    D) 45 minutes

And where, in 1979, did this take place?

    A) California
    B) North Wales
    C) Darwin, Australia
    D) Cherrapunji, India

100

101

102

103 About how many major earthquakes are there across the Earth every year?

    A) 19
    B) 12
    C) 16
    D) 25

104 In which country did the largest earthquake ever recorded occur in 1960?

    A) Japan
    B) Greece
    C) Chile
    D) USA

105 What was the magnitude of this earthquake?

    A) 9.5
    B) 9.6
    C) 9.7
    D) 9.9

And how large an area did this earthquake affect?

A) 225 by 50 miles/362 by 81 km
B) 350 by 60 miles/564 by 97 km
C) 525 by 80 miles/845 x 129 km
D) 750 by 100 miles/1208 by 161 km

What is the name for a minor quake that occurs before the main one?

A) Aftershock
B) Foreshock
C) Tremor
D) Preshock

On March 28, 1964, a massive earthquake with a 9.2 magnitude shook which US state?

A) Oregon
B) Alaska
C) California
D) Washington

Awesome Earthquakes

109

Earthquakes are most likely to occur in:
- **A)** Hot weather
- **B)** Cold weather
- **C)** Any weather - it makes no difference
- **D)** Wet weather

110

On what scale is the magnitude of an earthquake measured?
- **A)** Kelvin
- **B)** Fujita
- **C)** Richter
- **D)** Kitchen

111

If you find yourself indoors during an earthquake, is it usually best to:
- **A)** Rush outside
- **B)** Stay inside
- **C)** Stand on your head
- **D)** Panic

Awesome Earthquakes

112

What is the minimum magnitude for a quake to be defined as a major earthquake?

A) 6.0
B) 7.0
C) 8.0
D) 9.0

113

At least how many major earthquakes have there been in California in the last 200 years?

A) 3
B) 8
C) 11
D) 18

114

The border near Arkansas and Missouri was the site of an extraordinary series of earthquakes in 1811 and 1812 that included four major earthquakes. What strange effect did these earthquakes have?

A) The Mississippi River flowed backwards for a couple of hours
B) The state border was permanently moved
C) Dead people were seen walking around
D) A new mountain range was formed

Awesome Earthquakes

115

Which US state has had the most major earthquakes in the last 30 years?

- **A)** California
- **B)** Hawaii
- **C)** Florida
- **D)** Alaska

116

On what scale is the amount of damage caused by an earthquake measured?

- **A)** Mercator Scale
- **B)** Mercalli Scale
- **C)** Mulder Scale
- **D)** Mohs Scale

117

If an earthquake has an intensity, on this damage scale, of 12 how much damage does it cause?

- **A)** Almost total destruction
- **B)** Major structural damage to buildings
- **C)** Some structural damage to buildings
- **D)** Minor damage to plates, glassware, and so on

What instrument is used to measure an earthquake's intensity on the damage scale?

118

    A) Seismograph

    B) Oscilloscope

    C) Spirograph

    D) No instrument - scientists simply use observations and historical records

---

According to the US Geological Survey's National Earthquake Information Center (NEIC), global earthquake activity in recent years has been:

119

    A) Much the same

    B) Increasing

    C) Decreasing

    D) Increasingly erratic

The deadliest earthquake on record occurred way back in 1556 in which country?

120

    A) India

    B) Japan

    C) China

    D) Pakistan

121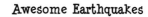

What is the minimum number of people who are estimated to have died in this earthquake?

A) 650,000
B) 780,000
C) 830,000
D) 900,000

122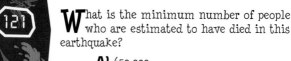

Approximately how many people died as a result of the Great San Francisco earthquake of 1906?

A) 3,000
B) 30,000
C) 300,000
D) 300

123

What caused the largest number of these deaths?

A) The fires that swept across the city for four days afterwards
B) Collapsing buildings and falling debris
C) A tsunami that hit the city from the Pacific Ocean
D) A cholera epidemic caused by pollution of the city's water supply

How do flash floods differ from other types of flood?

    A) They happen very quickly
    B) They are always accompanied by thunder and lightning
    C) They only affect coastal areas
    D) They only occur alongside rivers

How deep must flood water become before the average automobile is swept away?

    A) 2 feet/0.6 meters
    B) 3 feet/0.9 meters
    C) 1 foot/0.3 meters
    D) 4 feet/1.2 meters

Flash floods are often caused by which of these?

    A) A blocked drain
    B) Fault lines
    C) High tides
    D) Slow-moving thunderstorms

127 What is the most important thing to do if you are caught in a flash flood?

A) Get to higher ground as soon as possible

B) Collect all your most treasured possessions and put them in a suitcase

C) Dive into the nearest ditch

D) Start building a raft

128 What is a flood watch?

A) A device you wear on your wrist to tell you when a flood is due

B) A warning that floods have been reported

C) A team of people whose job it is to watch floods developing

D) An announcement from the authorities that a flood is possible

129 What percentage of flood deaths occur in vehicles?

A) 30%

B) 50%

C) 80%

D) 90%

Fearsome Floods

In which season of the year are floods most common?

130

- **A)** Winter
- **B)** Spring
- **C)** Summer
- **D)** Fall

Flash flood waters can move fast enough to roll boulders, tear out trees, and destroy buildings and bridges. This process is known as:

131

- **A)** Erasing
- **B)** Terminating
- **C)** Scouring
- **D)** Squelching

How big an area was covered by the great Mississippi River Flood of 1993?

132

- **A)** 400 miles/644 km long by 100 miles/161 km wide
- **B)** 500 miles/805 km long by 200 miles wide/322 km
- **C)** 600 miles/966 km long by 200 miles/322 km wide
- **D)** 500 miles/805 km long by 100 miles/161 km wide

133 And how many homes were damaged by this flood?

A) Over 100,000
B) Over 30,000
C) Over 50,000
D) Over 50,000

134 How deep does fast-moving flood water have to be to knock the average person off their feet?

A) 6 inches/15 cm
B) 1 foot/30 cm
C) 18 inches/45 cm
D) 2 feet/60 cm

135 The great majority of people killed in flash floods are:

A) Children
B) Citizens over 60
C) Males
D) Females

Fearsome Floods

What percentage of all presidential-declared natural disasters in the USA involve flooding?

    A) 25%
    B) 50%
    C) 75%
    D) 90%

Coastal floods are sometimes caused by what?

    A) Paved streets
    B) Solar flares
    C) Hurricanes
    D) Tourists

Over 6,000 people died in a flood in Galveston, Texas in September 1900. What type of flood was responsible?

    A) Flash flood
    B) Ice-jam flood
    C) Storm surge flood
    D) Dam-failure flood

139

Hurricanes and typhoons are regionally specific names for a strong weather system known as a:

A) Tropical storm
B) Tropical disaster
C) Tropical disturbance
D) Tropical cyclone

140

A tropical cyclone is defined as a tropical storm when it reaches what speed?

A) 35 mph/56 kph
B) 39 mph/63 kph
C) 45 mph/72 kph
D) 49 mph/79 kph

141

And what is the minimum speed for it to be defined as a hurricane?

A) 68 mph/109 kph
B) 73 mph/118 kph
C) 78 mph/126 kph
D) 80 mph/129 kph

Storms and Hurricanes

As well as tropical cyclones, there is another type of cyclone which generally forms within the belt of westerly winds encircling the globe between latitudes 30° S and 70° S. By what name are these (usually less damaging) cyclones known?

- **A)** Anti-cyclones
- **B)** Depression cyclones
- **C)** Mid-latitude cyclones
- **D)** Cyclones lite

What is the center of a hurricane called?

- **A)** Nose
- **B)** Stomach
- **C)** Mouth
- **D)** Eye

Hurricanes have different names according to where they occur. What are they called when they appear over the western Pacific Ocean?

- **A)** Hurricanes
- **B)** Typhoons
- **C)** Cyclones
- **D)** Tornadoes

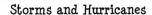

145 **A**nd what are they called in the Indian Ocean?

- **A)** Hurricanes
- **B)** Tornadoes
- **C)** Typhoons
- **D)** Cyclones

146 **W**hich areas of the world have the most hurricanes?

- **A)** Areas near the Equator
- **B)** Areas near the poles
- **C)** Areas near the Pacific Ocean
- **D)** Areas near the Indian Ocean

147 **W**hen is the main hurricane season in the North Atlantic?

- **A)** May to September
- **B)** July to December
- **C)** June to November
- **D)** August to January

Storms and Hurricanes

Which of these is a major cause of hurricane formation?

A) Bad thunderstorms

B) Sudden rise in atmospheric pressure

C) Warm ocean water

D) Jet aircraft

148

What does a hurricane hunter do?

A) Flies a plane and watches for a hurricane to form

B) Flies a plane into a hurricane to find out more about it

C) Follows a hurricane so that everyone knows where it is

D) Wears a cool aviator suit and poses a lot for photographers

149

The wind energy alone produced by an average hurricane is equivalent to:

A) The total electricity required to power a small town

B) Half the world's electrical generating capacity

C) The total electricity required by a city the size of Chicago

D) The energy released by ten H-bombs exploding

150

151 **W**hat is a storm surge?

- **A)** Severe flooding caused by higher than normal tides
- **B)** The combination of strong winds and heavy rain
- **C)** Spiraling air which rises and creates rain bands
- **D)** The sick feeling you get when you know that a hurricane is coming

152 **W**hat causes the most deaths from hurricanes?

- **A)** High winds
- **B)** Falling trees and buildings
- **C)** Storm surge
- **D)** Stress

153 **I**n 1998 Hurricane Mitch, the most destructive to strike the Western Hemisphere in the last 200 years, hit the countries of Central America. How many people were left dead or missing during the six days that it raged?

- **A)** 12,047
- **B)** 25,432
- **C)** 15,359
- **D)** 18,207

Most hurricanes last about a week. Hurricane John in 1994 holds the record for the longest lasting. How many days did it continue?

A) 19
B) 26
C) 31
D) 42

Where are the worst winds in a hurricane found?

A) Around the outside edges of the hurricane
B) Inside the eye of the hurricane
C) The eyewall around the eye of the hurricane
D) Behind the hurricane

The intensity of hurricanes is measured on what scale?

A) Beaufort Scale
B) Saffir-Sampson Scale
C) Blowers Scale
D) Fujita Scale

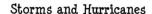

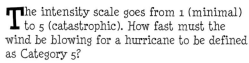

157

The intensity scale goes from 1 (minimal) to 5 (catastrophic). How fast must the wind be blowing for a hurricane to be defined as Category 5?

A) Over 155 mph/250 kph
B) Over 140 mph/225 kph
C) Over 125 mph/201 kph
D) Over 170 mph/274 kph

158

Which of these hurricanes was a Category 5?

A) Hurricane Fran (1996)
B) Hurricane Betsy (1965)
C) Hurricane Camille (1969)
D) Hurricane Earl (1998)

159

What is the average annual damage caused by hurricanes in the USA every year?

A) $2,080 million
B) $4,900 million
C) $3,800 million
D) $5,700 million

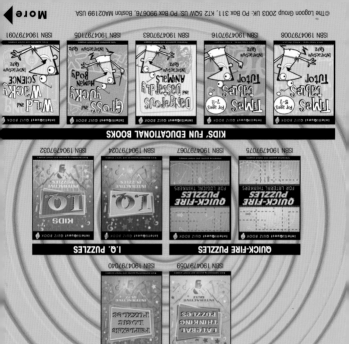

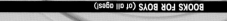

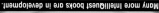

Hurricane names associated with particularly severe hurricanes are 'retired.' Which of the following hurricane names will never be used again for this reason?

A) Roxanne
B) Sam
C) Victor
D) Wanda

On which side of a hurricane are the strongest winds normally found (all directions are with reference to the hurricane's direction of movement)?

A) In front
B) Behind
C) Left
D) Right

Compared with the periphery, is the air pressure at the center of a hurricane:

A) Much the same
B) Much higher
C) It varies
D) Much lower

163 What is the main difference between tornadoes and hurricanes?

A) Tornadoes cause more death and destruction

B) Tornadoes move faster than hurricanes

C) Tornadoes cover a smaller area than hurricanes

D) The wind speed in a tornado is higher than in a hurricane

---

164 What is the scale used to measure the intensity of tornadoes?

A) Beaufort Scale

B) Richter Scale

C) Kelvin Scale

D) Fujita Scale

---

165 By what other name are tornadoes often called?

A) Winders

B) Creepers

C) Jivers

D) Twisters

Terrifying Tornadoes

166 One of the biggest areas for tornadoes is the area above the Mid-Western United States, which includes Kansas, Nebraska, Iowa, Oklahoma, and Texas. What term is commonly used to describe this region?

A) Twister Bay
B) Tornado Alley
C) Blowout Corner
D) Dead Man's Trail

167 At about what time of day is the formation of a tornado most likely?

A) Midnight to 6 a.m.
B) 6 a.m. to noon
C) Noon to 3 p.m.
D) 3 p.m. to 6 p.m.

168 In what year was the first tornado accurately predicted before it struck?

A) 1948
B) 1974
C) 1953
D) 1965

169

By what name is a tornado over water usually called?

    A) Water chute
    B) Water spout
    C) Typhoon
    D) Monsoon

170

With improved methods of predicting tornadoes, deaths are generally less common nowadays. In what year was the last tornado which caused over 80 deaths?

    A) 1948
    B) 1961
    C) 1955
    D) 1968

171

And where did this take place?
    A) Flint, Michigan
    B) Tupelo, Mississippi
    C) Udall, Kansas
    D) Gainsville, Georgia

Although tornadoes occur worldwide, the greatest concentration is in the United States. About how many tornadoes are formed here in an average year?

    A) 800
    B) 450
    C) 200
    D) 1,200

In what month do the greatest number of tornado deaths occur in the United States?

    A) May
    B) June
    C) July
    D) August

Which of the following celebrities, as an infant, survived a tornado that killed over 200 people?

    A) Jodie Foster
    B) Harrison Ford
    C) Elvis Presley
    D) Angelina Jolie

172

173

174

175 Most tornadoes in the Northern Hemisphere travel in which direction?

A) East to West
B) North to South
C) Southwest to Northeast
D) Southeast to Northwest

176 Which of the following towns was hit by a tornado on three consecutive years from 1916 to 1918, each time on the exact same date, May 20th?

A) Lazbuddie, Texas
B) Codell, Kansas
C) Enid, Oklahoma
D) Tupelo, Mississippi

177 Which US state has the highest number of deaths caused by tornadoes?

A) Kansas
B) Texas
C) Alabama
D) Arkansas

In what direction do tornadoes in the Northern Hemisphere rotate?

178

A) Nobody knows
B) Mostly clockwise
C) Mostly counterclockwise
D) About equal

In 1930 a man was picked up by a tornado but did not survive to tell the tale. How far was he carried?

179

A) 4 km/2.5 miles
B) 2 km/1.25 miles
C) 1 km/0.6 miles
D) 0.5 km/0.3 miles

A funnel cloud is also a column of violently rotating winds extending down from a thunderstorm but what is the difference between a tornado and a funnel cloud?

180

A) Funnel clouds only last a matter of seconds
B) There is no difference
C) Funnel clouds travel more slowly
D) Funnel clouds don't touch the earth

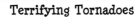

181 **W**hat is the average speed of a tornado?

A) 20 mph/32 kph
B) 35 mph/56 kph
C) 50 mph/81 kph
D) 90 mph/145 kph

182 **W**hat is the longest continuous tornado track in recorded history?

A) 42 miles/68 km
B) 117 miles/188 km
C) 219 miles/353 km
D) 312 miles/502 km

183 **T**he Pampa, Texas tornado is cited as moving the heaviest thing in tornado records, which was what?

A) A house weighing in excess of 50,000 pounds
B) Machinery weighing more that 30,000 pounds
C) A truck weighing 5000 pounds
D) A herd of cows weighing about 20,000 pounds

Springs and Geysers

A geyser is a hole in the ground that releases bursts of steam and hot water. What three things are needed for a geyser to work?

A) Water, electricity and pressure
B) Water, pressure and money
C) Water, gas and heat
D) Water, heat and pressure

184

Where are over half the geysers in the whole world to be found?

A) Northern Chile
B) Rotorua, New Zealand
C) Yellowstone National Park
D) Jellystone Park

185

Steam from geysers often smells like:

A) Unwashed socks
B) Earl Grey tea
C) Crushed sage
D) Rotten eggs

186

187 Old Faithful is the name of the most famous geyser in Yellowstone National Park. How often (on average) does it erupt?

    A) Every 78 minutes
    B) Every 45 minutes
    C) Every 20 minutes
    D) Every now and then

188 And how high is the fountain when it erupts?

    A) 70 feet/21.3 meters
    B) 150 feet/30.5 meters
    C) 120 feet/36.6 meters
    D) 100 feet/45.7 meters

189 What is a fumarole?

    A) A steam vent spewing gases out of the ground
    B) A very bad smell
    C) A small particle ejected when a geyser erupts
    D) A French cigarette

Springs and Geysers

Which country generates 87% of its power from geothermal energy, mainly hot springs and geysers?

    A) New Zealand
    B) Canada
    C) Iceland
    D) USA

The Steamboat Geyser in Yellowstone Park is the highest currently erupting natural geyser, reaching heights of up to how far?

    A) 300 feet/91 meters
    B) 200 feet/61 meters
    C) 400 feet/122 meters
    D) 100 feet/45.7 meters

Which of these countries does not have any active geysers?

    A) Egypt
    B) Bolivia
    C) Peru
    D) Japan

193 Up to what temperature have living organisms been found in hot springs?

A) 65° C/149° F
B) 75° C/167° F
C) 85° C/185° F
D) 95° C/203° F

194 Which of these can cause a geyser to stop working?

A) Earth movements
B) Building of geothermal power plants
C) Litter being thrown down them
D) All of these

195 The name geyser comes from an Icelandic word meaning:

A) Heat
B) Scald
C) Gush
D) Water

Springs and Geysers

196

What do the geysers Riverside, Castle and Great Fountain have in common?

- **A)** All in Yellowstone Park
- **B)** All man-made
- **C)** All now inactive
- **D)** All in New Zealand

197

Where would you find the world's highest geyser field, at 4,300 meters above sea level?

- **A)** Siberia
- **B)** Chile
- **C)** USA
- **D)** Argentina

198

The mineral Rhyolite is high in silica and performs what vital plumbing element with regard to geysers?

- **A)** Creates a water-tight seal along the geyser walls
- **B)** Purifies the water
- **C)** Allows water to leak through and lowers pressure
- **D)** Allows water to cool down

199 The hole in the ozone layer is believed to have been caused by the release of which gas or gases?

A) Carbon dioxide
B) Propane and butane
C) Chlorofluorocarbons
D) Sulfur dioxide

200 Why is the ozone layer important?

A) It blocks harmful ultraviolet radiation from the Sun
B) It makes everyone feel nice and fresh
C) It reflects radio waves, allowing broadcasts to travel long distances
D) It vaporises most meteorites before they can fall to Earth and cause damage

201 Above which area of the Earth is the biggest hole in the ozone layer?

A) Pacific Ocean
B) Australasia
C) Antarctic
D) Arctic Circle

Environment and Pollution

202

This hole in the ozone layer is roughly equal in size to which country?

A) Iceland
B) USA
C) Australia
D) Mexico

203

What are the main acids in acid rain?
A) Nitric acid and acetic acid
B) Sulfuric acid and nitric acid
C) Sulfuric acid and hydrochloric acid
D) Nitric acid and hydrochloric acid

204

What is the main cause of acid rain?
A) Water pollution
B) Chlorofluorocarbons
C) Burning fossil fuels
D) Electrical storms

205 Certain gases in our atmosphere trap heat from the sun, causing the Earth's temperature to rise. What is the popular term used to describe this?

A) Hothouse effect
B) Glasshouse effect
C) Greenhouse effect
D) Funhouse effect

206 Which of these is NOT a greenhouse gas?

A) Carbon dioxide
B) Nitrogen
C) Methane
D) Nitrous oxide

207 How have human beings altered the composition of the Earth's atmosphere?

A) They have polluted it with excess ozone
B) They have polluted it with carbon dioxide gas
C) They have made the atmospheric pressure drop
D) They have made the atmospheric temperature drop

Environment and Pollution

What US city is generally considered to have America's worst air pollution problem?

    A) Chicago
    B) New York
    C) Los Angeles
    D) Houston

Most scientists now believe that the greenhouse gases produced by human activity are causing global warming. By how much do scientists expect the Earth's overall temperature to rise in the next fifty years?

    A) 1.0 to 3.0° C
    B) 0.5 to 1.0° C
    C) 0.2 to 0.8° C
    D) 2.0 to 5.0° C

What would be the effect of such a rise in global temperatures?

    A) Floods
    B) Droughts
    C) Storms and hurricanes
    D) All of these

208

209

210

211 What is the main cause of water pollution in unindustrialized nations?

A) Pesticides
B) Untreated sewage
C) Industrial chemicals
D) Vehicle emissions

212 Before lead was banned from gasoline in the industrialized world, it was a major cause of air pollution. What percentage of children in the USA are estimated to have had their intelligence damaged by atmospheric lead pollution?

A) 17%
B) 10%
C) 5%
D) 25%

213 Since the virtual abolition of leaded gas in the USA, by how much has the mean blood-lead level of the American population reduced?

A) Over 35%
B) Over 50%
C) Over 60%
D) Over 75%

Violent Volcanoes

Mount St. Helens, in Washington, is one link in a chain of volcanoes known as:

    A) The Ring of Fire
    B) The Vulcan's Lair
    C) The Devil's Bowels
    D) The Serpent's Tail

How hot can the molten lava in a volcano become?

    A) 1,200° F/649° C
    B) 1,800° F/982° C
    C) 2,140° F/1171° C
    D) 5,000° F/2760° C

Which of these continents has no active volcanoes?

    A) Europe
    B) Asia
    C) Australia
    D) Antarctica

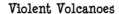

Violent Volcanoes

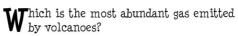

217 **W**hich is the most abundant gas emitted by volcanoes?

- **A)** Water vapor
- **B)** Sulfur dioxide
- **C)** Carbon dioxide
- **D)** Laughing gas

218 **W**hich volcano is famous for burying the Roman cities of Pompeii and Herculaneum?

- **A)** Mount Etna
- **B)** Mount Vesuvius
- **C)** Stromboli
- **D)** Mount Nero

219 **W**hat are scientists who study volcanoes called?

- **A)** Vulcanologists
- **B)** Seismologists
- **C)** Vulcans
- **D)** Cool dudes

Violent Volcanoes

What is a volcano that erupts once in hundreds of years then goes back to sleep called?

    A) Dormant
    B) Extinct
    C) Active
    D) Dead

What do the largest volcanic eruptions cause?

    A) Global warming
    B) Terrible headaches
    C) Holes in the ozone layer
    D) Global cooling

Which is reckoned to have been the loudest-ever volcanic eruption?

    A) Krakatoa
    B) Mount Etna
    C) Mount Vesuvius
    D) Uncle Pete after his Christmas dinner

Violent Volcanoes

About how many active volcanoes are there on land?

- **A)** 1,200
- **B)** 300
- **C)** 900
- **D)** 600

Which is the world's largest active volcano?

- **A)** Tambora
- **B)** Mount St. Helens
- **C)** Mauna Loa
- **D)** Mount Vesuvius

Materials ejected from a volcano that include dust, ash, cinders, pumice, and blocks are collectively termed...

- **A)** Volcano vomit
- **B)** Tephra
- **C)** Magma
- **D)** Roadkill

Which US state has the most volcanoes?

226

- **A)** Washington
- **B)** Hawaii
- **C)** Alaska
- **D)** Texas

Which country has the largest number of active volcanoes?

227

- **A)** USA
- **B)** Indonesia
- **C)** Belgium
- **D)** Japan

What are created when large volcanoes collapse?

228

- **A)** Ignimbrites
- **B)** Archipelagoes
- **C)** Bowling alleys
- **D)** Calderas

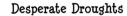

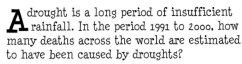

229

A drought is a long period of insufficient rainfall. In the period 1991 to 2000, how many deaths across the world are estimated to have been caused by droughts?

- **A)** Over 200,000
- **B)** Over 150,000
- **C)** Over 100,000
- **D)** Over 250,000

230

Africa's worst dry spell in the last 100 years occurred in 1991-92. How big an area did it cover?

- **A)** 1.4 million square miles/ 2.3 million square km
- **B)** 1.7 million square miles 2.7 million square km
- **C)** 2.6 million square miles 4.2 million square km
- **D)** 2.1 million square miles 3.4 million square km

231

And how many people did it affect?

- **A)** 20 million
- **B)** 32 million
- **C)** 28 million
- **D)** 24 million

Desperate Droughts

Many droughts in the southern hemisphere are caused by an ocean phenomenon called:

A) Ring of Fire
B) Gulf Stream
C) El Niño
D) Jet Stream

232

On average, how often does this phenomenon occur?

A) Every five years
B) Every two years
C) Every four years
D) Every ten years

233

A series of terrible droughts affected the United States in the 1930s. What collective term was used to describe them?

A) Dust Storm
B) Dust Vase
C) Dust Jacket
D) Dust Bowl

234

235

What percentage of the United States was affected by these droughts in the worst year?

    A) 40%
    B) 70%
    C) 50%
    D) 80%

236

The 1987-89 drought was the most expensive natural disaster of any kind ever to affect the USA. What was the estimated total cost of this drought to the US economy?

    A) $28 billion
    B) $39 billion
    C) $46 billion
    D) $51 billion

237

In a drought with desert-like temperatures of over 100 degrees Fahrenheit what is the longest a person can hope to survive?

    A) 1 day
    B) 2 days
    C) 3 days
    D) 4 days

What is the total water supply of the world?

238

A) 186 million cubic miles/
299 million cubic km

B) 245 million cubic miles/
394 million cubic km

C) 298 million cubic miles/
480 million cubic km

D) 326 million cubic miles/
525 million cubic km

What is the highest temperature ever measured on Earth?

239

A) 55° C/131° F
B) 58° C/136° F
C) 61° C/142° F
D) 63° C/145° F

And where was this temperature recorded?

240

A) Browning, Montana
B) Death Valley, California
C) Dallol, Ethiopia
D) Al'Aziziyah, Libya

241

How many tons of space dust are estimated to fall on the Earth every year?

    A) 3,000
    B) 300
    C) 30
    D) 3

242

If you are standing on the Equator, at about what speed is the Earth revolving under you?

    A) 500 mph/805 kph
    B) 1,500 mph/2415 kph
    C) 1,000 mph/1610 kph
    D) 2,000 mph/3220 kph

243

How many different sorts of fog are there?

    A) 4
    B) 2
    C) 6
    D) 1

What is the name of the largest known impact crater on the Earth?

244

A) Barringer Crater
B) Vredefort Ring
C) Clearwater Lakes craters
D) Caloris basin

What weather-related reason is the leading cause of aircraft accidents?

245

A) Reduced visibility due to snow/rain
B) Microbursts (wind blasts)
C) Updrafts (upward air currents)
D) Tornadoes

What is lightning on the fringes of space called?

246

A) Green elves
B) Green flash
C) Green strike
D) Green goblins

247 Which is the warmest ocean?
- **A)** Atlantic
- **B)** Pacific
- **C)** Indian
- **D)** Arctic

248 And which is the warmest sea?
- **A)** Sea of Japan
- **B)** Dead Sea
- **C)** Sargasso Sea
- **D)** Red Sea

249 Due to continental drift, North America and Europe are moving apart at an average speed of:
- **A)** 3 meters/9.8 feet per year
- **B)** 30 cm/1 foot per year
- **C)** 3 cm/1.2 in per year
- **D)** 30 meters/98 feet per year

What is the name of the mysterious phenomenon which is caused by earth tremors that are too weak to be felt, but sounds like a distant cannon, especially on or near the water?

A) Ghost fire
B) Shadow fire
C) Barisal guns
D) Bad vibes

250

What kind of fog forms when cold air blows against warm water or warm air blows against cold water?

A) Radiation fog
B) Steam fog
C) Advection fog
D) Valley fog

251

Of all the animal species that have ever lived on Earth, what percentage is still living on the planet today?

A) 10%
B) 20%
C) 30%
D) 40%

252

253 What is the highest wind gust ever to be recorded on land?

- **A)** 170 mph/274 kph
- **B)** 186 mph/299 kph
- **C)** 231 mph/372 kph
- **D)** 207 mph/333 kph

254 And where did it take place?

- **A)** Goa, India
- **B)** Mount Washington, New Hampshire
- **C)** Annapurna Mountains, Nepal
- **D)** Mount Erebus, Antarctica

255 What is the hottest place on Earth, when looking at the average temperature?

- **A)** Dallol, Ethiopia
- **B)** Al'Aziziyah, Libya
- **C)** Browning, Montana
- **D)** Houston, Texas

And what is the coldest place on Earth, again looking at the average temperature?

A) Reykjavic, Iceland
B) Kiruna, Sweden
C) Vladivostok, Russia
D) Plateau Station, Antarctica

256

Which sea is so salty you can literally lie on it and read a book without sinking?

A) Red Sea
B) Caspian Sea
C) North Sea
D) Dead Sea

257

What is the deepest known point in the ocean, reaching depths of over 36,000 feet/10,976 meters?

A) Aleutian Trench
B) Puerto Rico Trench
C) Mariana Trench
D) French Trench

258

259

What is the name used to describe the level below the Earth's surface at which the ground becomes saturated with water?

A) Water line
B) Water gate
C) Water cooler
D) Water table

260

Which two metals make up the Earth's inner core?

A) Iron and steel
B) Iron and aluminum
C) Copper and iron
D) Nickel and iron

261

Up to how hot is the Earth's inner core believed to be?

A) 1,000° C/1832° F
B) 7,200° C/12992° F
C) 5,600° C/10112° F
D) 3,800° C/6872° F

This is roughly equal to the temperature of:

    A) A pizza straight out of the oven
    B) The flame from a welder's blowtorch
    C) The inside of a blast furnace
    D) The surface of the Sun

262

Which city has the deepest underground subway station in the world, at 97 meters/318 feet below ground?

    A) Moscow
    B) London
    C) New York
    D) Tokyo

263

In which area has an underground coal seam been burning for at least 1,000 years?

    A) Snowdonia, North Wales
    B) Wingen, Australia
    C) Kuzbass, Russia
    D) Pennsylvania, USA

264

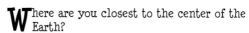

265 **W**here are you closest to the center of the Earth?

    A) The Galapagos Islands
    B) Nepal
    C) The North Pole
    D) New York

266 **T**he Russians began digging the world's deepest hole in 1970. How far down have they got?

    A) 72 km/45 miles
    B) 36 km/22 miles
    C) 12 km/7.5 miles
    D) Only they know

267 **T**he Earth's crust is made up of huge, thick plates sitting on top of the softer, underlying mantle. How deep are these plates?

    A) 50-250 miles/80-403 km
    B) 250-1,000 miles/403-1610 km
    C) Over 1,000 miles/1610 km
    D) Less than 50 miles/80 km

Up and Under

The Earth's plates are constantly moving. What is their estimated speed?

268

A) 1-10 cm/0.4-4 inches per year
B) 10-100 cm/4-40 inches per year
C) 1-10 meters/3.3-33 feet per year
D) 10-100 meters/33-328 feet per year

The movement of the Earth's plates is responsible for which of these phenomena?

269

A) Global warming
B) Atmospheric pollution
C) Continental drift
D) Bad TV reception

When two continental plates collide, what is the likeliest result?

270

A) Earthquakes
B) Volcanoes
C) Mountain ranges
D) Plagues of locusts

Other Titles

There are many other exciting quiz
and puzzle books in the IntelliQuest range,
and your QUIZMO electronic unit
knows the answers to them all!

You can order from your
local bookshop or on-line bookseller.

For a full listing of current titles
(and ISBN numbers) see:

www.intelliquestbooks.com

LAGOON
BOOKS